The top Biblical stories of Old Testament - easy to read and understand Old Testament Bible History

Written by Winslow P. Hill

Introduction

Listed here are the top 40 stories of the Bible old testament in an easy to read & understand format, I wrote this brief history of the Bible for my own purpose and for my children to read because I saw they did not know the basic stories of the Bible OT. There is an ancient wisdom in these words a History that ties us all together with past, present, and future to show us how to live our lives and to get the most enjoyment and fulfillment from it. Our creator gave us this book of wisdom to help us understand the mysteries of our lives and others. To everything there is a time and a season, this is our season for Wisdom, Health and Favor you need only to understand and it will be all tied together.

These stories are not ranked like a top 40+ list but just that they are worth knowing to gain knowledge from. I have them in chronological order. Please read and learn what you can because it is for our benefit that we know these stories and understand them. I just wanted to make it as easy to read and to understand as possible the old biblical stories of antiquity.

Table of Contents

22.	David's was a man after God' own Heart

23.	City of David

24.	Solomon's Wisdom & Favor

25.	Solomon the builder

26.	Kings of Israel and Juda

27.	Daniel Favor and Great health

28.	Daniel and the interpretation

29.	Daniel and the Lion's den

30.	Nebuchadnezzar's makes a statue

31.	Queen Esther Highly Favored

32.	Esther Time had come for her purpose to be revealed

1 Adam & Eve's Promise

God created Adam the first Man and then made Eve his wife

Satan gave Eve an Apple from the Tree of Life in the Garden of Eden which God forbid them to eat

Eve ate the apple and then gave it to Adam to eat and they gained knowledge of good and evil

They were then cast out of the Garden of Eden to wander the Earth for that sin

Adam and Eve first had their sons Kane and Able

Eve had the promise from God to end sin through a son, and then Kane killed Able

God promised Eve's child will save the world from her original sin someday (the eating of the Apple)

2 Cain and Able

Cain and Able were first two sons of Adam and Eve

Cain was the first born was a farmer

Abel was a shepherd

The both made sacrifices to the Lord and Able's was pleasing to God he gave his best from his flock

Cain's sacrifice was not pleasing because he did not give of his first fruits, his best

Cain was jealous of able and killed him in the field

God came looking for Able and found his blood in the field and him dead

The Lord ask Cain what happened to Able? Cain said I am not my brother's keeper

The Lord said Able's blood cries out to him from the field and he knew he was murdered.

God cursed Cain and banished him from the land but put a mark on him, so no one would harm him

Adam and Eve then had another son Seth who would be the father of Enosh.

Who was the father of Kenan.

Who was the father of Mahalalel.

Who was the father of Jared.

Who was the father of Enoch.

Who was the father of Methuselah.

Who was the father of Lamech.

Who was the father of Noah.

Through Noah the promise will be keep through his son Seth (The Semites)

The promise child will come from Seth, Abraham is in the line of Seth

Through Abraham a promise was given that his descendants would be as numerous as the stars and a child Isaac was given to Abraham and Sarah

Through Isaac Jacob (also known as Israel) was born. Joseph was a son of Israel

Joseph was sold to slavery and went down to Egypt

From Egypt Israel was saved from famine through Joseph being appointed Prime Minster of Egypt

Out of Egypt with God's help Moses freed the Israelites

To Moses the Ten Commandments and law was given by God

Moses led the Israelites to the promise land

David a king in Israel is born and a promise is given.

David's son will always sit on God's thrown

Jesus's Earthly Father Joseph is a direct descendant of King David

Mary and Joseph have the promise child in Bethlehem

Jesus dies for all our sins on the cross at Calvary

Eve's promise from God is fulfilled and we are no longer under the law.

3 Noah's Times & The Flood

Noah was son of Lamech

When Noah was five hundred years old, he became a father

His sons; Ham, Japheth, & Shem (father of Semites" the Jews "it is where the word anti-Semite comes from, Abraham would be his direct descendant)

It was a dark time for Mankind and men only chased their own desires

So, God wished to destroy the world and rebuild with the only just Man he could find, Noah

So, God had Noah build an ark

He told Noah about the up coming flood that would destroy the world

Noah followed God with Blind faith and built the giant ark

He then filled it with two of every kind of animal male and female

Then rains came and flooded the world for forty days and forty nights

Noah was a drift for many days

Then he sent out a dove to find land and it returned empty

But the second time it returned with an olive branch the flood water had rescinded

They found land at last and settled with his wife and his 3 sons and their wives.

Noah built a vineyard and got Drunk after this long ordeal

Ham found him naked and ran to tell his brothers

His brothers would not shame their father, so they backed in with a blanket and covered his body

When he awoke he found out Ham told everyone, so he cursed him and said he would serve Shem forever

Noah story ends here but we no that through God's Grace Shem lines live on and Abraham father of many nations will be a direct descendent of God's grace to Noah's Family.

4 Abraham's Righteousness

God made Abraham a promise his people would be as numerous as the stars in the heavens

Abraham believed it and it was counted to him as righteousness from God

God also promised Abraham the promised Land modern day Israel, but he must leave his Father's family and go alone with his wife and servants to occupy the land

But Abraham took his nephew Lot because he did not have an heir

Abraham was blessed and his flocks along with Lot's grew in great size

Lot and Abraham had to seperate and Abraham let Lot chose the land he wanted, so he chose the better land the fertile planes of Sodom and Gomorrah

Lot was taken prisoner and had to be saved by Abraham and his men

Lot then lived in Sodom and Gomorrah the people did evil things there

God came to Abraham and told him he would destroy Sodom and Gomorrah due to their wickedness, but Abraham bartered for Lot's life as well as any other Good man found there, but there was only Lot to be found

The Angels came to visit Lot and he welcomed them, but he told them to sleep in his house or they would be gang raped which was the Sodom way

The gangs came to Lot's door and demand he bring out the men to sodamize them (they did not know they were angels)

The angels Blinded the men and told Lot for him and his family to leave at once, Lot took his wife and two daughters and left the city as God rained down fire upon it.

Lot's wife turned around to look as was killed instantly

Lot then lived in a cave and his daughters thinking all the young men were dead, so they got him drunk and had sex with him and gave birth to two races of men that the Israelites have had problems with forever

This all stemmed from Abraham taking Lot to the promised land and not waiting for God's plan of a promised child as an heir

Not everyone can go where we are going we must trust God's Plan not everyone will be blessed the same, but we must accept our lot in life and enjoy the blessing & work we are given

There is an ancient wisdom here in the story of Abraham for all men and religions that is why Abraham is the father of many religions under one God of Abraham

5 Abraham's Promise

God promised Abraham a child

Sarah got in a hurry and gave her slave Hagar to Abraham and Ishmael was born to her servant Hagar by Abraham.

Ishmael was not the Promised child but a great nation he would become

God came to visit and told of the child Sarah would have, the promised child to Abraham

Sarah laughed because she was old

Sarah was 90 and Abraham was 100 when Isaac was born in their old age

Isaac was the promise child through him a great nation will come, which was Israel and change the world forever

6 Isaac & Jacob

Isaac had Jacob and Esau twins, but Esau was the elder

Jacob tricked Esau out of his birth right
for a bowl of stew one day when he
came in from Hunting and starving he
told Esau he would give him a bowl of
stew for his birth right

Esau said what good would a birthright
do me if I starve to death

Jacob tricked Isaac out of Esau's blessing
with the help of Rebecca his mother.

Jacob fled to his uncle Lehman worked 7
years for his wife Rachael and 7 more for
wife Leah they were daughters of
Lehman

On his way to Lehman he had a vision of
a latter with angels ascending and
descending from heaven to earth

Racheal was baron at first, but Leah had many sons and 1 daughter

Racheal then had Joseph, Jacob's favorite son and later died in childbirth giving birth to Benjamin.

God blessed Jacob in all he did, and he had 12 sons and 1 daughter.

Jacob worked for Lehman tending flocks and God blessed him with great numbers

Lehman changed Jacob's wages ten times and Finally he left

Jacob took his flocks, wives, and children and went home to meet Esau

Jacob meet Esau along the way and bowed down for forgiveness and they made their peace

Jacob would dwell in the promise land with his family

Jacob's twelve sons; Reuben, Simeon, Levi, Judah, Dan, Naphtali, Gad, Asher, Issachar, Zebulun, Joseph, and Benjamin. His only daughter Dinah. The twelve sons became the tribes of Israel

7 <u>Joseph's Favor</u>

Joseph was Israel first son to Rachael the wife that Jacob loved the most

Joseph had his father's favor and he gave him a coat of many colors

Joseph 10 brothers not of his Mother, were Jealous of him

Joseph had a dream his brothers would bow down to him one day he told his brothers of the dream and they were very Jealous of him

His Brothers plotted for a chance to get rid of him, so they would be favorites of Israel

Joseph brothers sold him into slavery; he ended up in Egypt working for an Egyptian named Pontifer

Joseph was falsely accused by Pontifer's wife of rape and placed in prison

Pharaoh's Baker and Cup Barer were in prison and Joseph interpreted their dreams

He said the Cup Barer would be lifted by Pharaoh and the Baker would die by Pharaoh's decree and it all came true

All Joseph did flourish because he had God's Favor

One day the Cup Barer remembered Joseph to Pharaoh when Pharaoh had bad dreams

Dream 1 was; from the Nile were coming up seven cows, of handsome appearance and robust flesh, and then seven other cows were coming up after them from the Nile of ugly appearance and lean of flesh, and they stood beside the cows which were on the Nile bank. And the cows of ugly appearance and lean of flesh devoured the seven good cows.

Dream 2 was; seven ears of grain were growing on one stalk, healthy and good. And seven ears of grain, thin and beaten by the east wind were growing up after them. And the thin ears of grain swallowed up the seven healthy and full ears of grain.

Joseph interpreted Pharaohs dreams that no one else could

The dream meant there would be 7 years of famine after 7 prosperous years

Joseph's advice to Pharaoh was to save the seven years of plenty to provide for the 7 years of famine.

Pharaoh put Joseph in charge of all Egypt because he was the wisest man of his time and it flourished with God's Favor.

All came to Egypt for food in the famine because Joseph wisely save grain for 7 years

Joseph was raised for just a time as this, to save his people

Joseph gained all of Egypt's Property for Pharaoh he was blessed and favored above all.

8 <u>Joseph's higher purpose</u>

Joseph brothers sold him into slavery for evil, but God had a higher purpose for good.

Joseph was sold to Pontifer as a slave, God blessed Joseph and he ran Pontifer his master's House & Estate

Joseph was falsely accused by Pontifers wife of rape and placed in Prison

Joseph was blessed with favor again and came to run the Prison

By interpreting Pharaoh's dreams
Joseph was again blessed and became
Prime minster of Egypt

God had Joseph rule Egypt for just such a time as this.

There was famine in Israel's land, and he sent his 10 sons to Egypt because there was food there

When Joseph 10 brothers came and meet with him, they did not recognize him, and he ask them questions

They said they were all brothers of same Father the youngest was at home

Joseph accused them of being spies, he was testing them to see if they changed

Joseph held one of his brothers till they returned with the younger his own brother Benjamin of his Mother Rachael

Joseph ordered their silver be put back in their sack with the grain

When the brothers returned home the told their father what had happen, but he would not send Benjamin to Egypt to meet Joseph

When Israel finality agreed because the food was gone the brothers returned to Egypt one more time with Benjamin

Joseph had his silver cup put in Benjamin's grain sack to test the other brothers, then he accused Benjamin of theft

This time Judah spoke up and offered his own life for Benjamin's as not to hurt their father again

This time Joseph could not contain himself he was overcome and revealed himself to his brothers

Joseph purpose was revealed to his Brothers they meant it for evil when they sold Joseph out of Jealousy as a slave, but God meant it to save Israel and all Egypt from famine

Joseph sent for his Father with Pharos's blessing

Israel went with all his family and livestock to Egypt to reside in the land of Goshen.

The Israelites would stay there for 400 years to the planned Deliverer would arrive "Moses"

Joseph died, and the new Pharaohs did not know him, and the Israelites became Egyptian slaves and stayed in bondage for 400 years

9 <u>Moses higher Purpose</u>

Moses was born in the time Pharaoh when he was having all the male child of Israel put to death

Moses Mother put him in a basket and sent him down the Nile

Baby Moses was found by Pharaoh's Daughter and named him Moses which means drawn from the water

Moses sister Miriam followed him and told Pharaoh's Sister Servants she knew a Nursemaid for him.

Moses's own Mother became his Nursemaid

Pharaoh's Sister raised him as her own

While in the Palace Moses was educated with the best the world had to offer

Moses served in Pharos army and learned how to rule and lead men

One day after Moses no doubted discovered he was Hebrew he killed to protect a slave from the task Master of the Hebrew slaves

Moses fled for his life to the land of
Midian.

Moses meets Jethro and his 7 daughters
in that land and became a sheep herder

Moses married Zephora Jethro's eldest
daughter and had 2 sons living in the
Shadow of Mt Sinai

One-day Moses saw a bush that burned
on Sinai and went to investigate

God said take off your shoes because
you stand on holy ground

God told him the plan for his life to lead
the Israelites out of Bondage.

Moses said he could not lead them he
was not eloquent enough he stuttered

God showed Moses he could, and he left for Egypt in an act of great faith

10 <u>Moses and Israelites A tale of two faiths</u>

Moses leaves his Mount Sanai and travels to Egypt

Moses meets with Pharaoh and tells him let my people go but Pharaoh's heart was hardened by God to show us what Great things God can do

Pharaoh resists and 10 plagues follow

1. Blood in the Nile River the river turns red

2. Frogs plague the land

3. Lice or gnats plague the land

4. Flies plague the land

5. Egyptian Livestock all die off

6. Boils plague the Egyptians

7. Hail that rains down that burns

8. Locust plague the land

9. Complete Darkness for 3 days in Egypt

10. The Final plague is the death of the first born of Egypt, Pharos own son dies

Moses tells the Israelites that they can be redeemed by the blood of a lamb over their door

The Lamb represents the son of God, Jesus

The Angel of death passes the Israelites by while killing the first born of Egypt

The Egyptians cry out over the death of their first born

Pharaoh lets the Israelites go and the leave Egypt with the Gold and possession of the Egyptians

This is all part of God's plan to raise them in the presence of their enemies

Once in the dessert Pharaoh's heart is hardened again and he pursues them to the Red Sea

Moses parts the Red Sea to escape and it then collapses on the pursuing Egyptians

In the Dessert Moses is giving the Ten Commandments and the Law for the foundation of God's Society

But some of the Israelites reject the law and make a Golden calf to worship.

God destroys them and the Levites rally to the lord's side to help Moses

Moses has Caleb and Joshua and 10 others scout out the Promised Land

The 10 say they cannot take because it is too hard and there are Giants living there

But Joshua and Caleb say it ours to take with the help of the Lord

All but Joshua and Caleb wonder the desert for 40 years and never enter the Promised Land for their lack of Faith

After 40 years Moses is called to his people and Joshua leads them into the Promise land

11 Moses youth renewed

Moses was called to lead his people out of slavery in Egypt at age 80

He was given by the Lord the basic Mosaic Laws that govern God's people and the Ten commandments

Moses led the Israelites through the desert for 40 years

Moses Father law Jethro came to visit and told Moses he should set up judges under him

He set judges over thousands, hundreds, and tens to take the responsibility off Moses

Moses only heard the very hard cases that could not be settled

Moses was said to have the energy of a young man doing his work for God

Moses lived to 120 his eyes not dimmed his natural strength not abated

Moses lead the Israelites to the Promised Land and then was called up on the mountain and gathered to his people

Joshua his aid would lead them into the Promised Land

12 Joshua's Faith

Joshua was around 80 years old when he took over for Moses

Joshua crossed the Jordan river and brought the Israelites into the promised land

Joshua followed God's plan for conquest of the promised land he was one of the world's great military leaders

Joshua leads the Israelites around the city of Jericho 7 times per God's plan.

On the 7th day they blew their horns and the walls came down

Nowhere else in the bible does this happen by blind faith

Joshua destroys the inhabitants of Jericho except for Rahab the prostitute who helped the Israeli spies escape the walls

Joshua then turned his attention to the city of AI

Joshua first attempt at AI failed because one of the Israelites took spoils from Jericho when God said not to

After that person who disobeyed God was punished with Death, they soon took AI and total destroyed it

Joshua was defeating all the armies he came up against in the name of the Lord's Favor and all in the land feared them

Joshua was then deceived by the Gibeonites who pretended to come from a far-off land to make a treaty

Joshua did not inquire of the Lord about the Gibeonites and was tricked into a treaty

The Gibeonites pretended to be from a far-off land by wearing dirty close and carrying old wine flasks and moldy bread to give the appearance they were not living in the promised land and could make a treaty with Joshua and not break God's rule that all other tribes had to be driven out of the promised land.

The Gibeonites descendants remain in the promise land to this day

Joshua then went on to destroy 5 more kings' armies in one day, 33 Kings in all

Joshua fought the Amorites in the Valley Ayalon and asked God to let the Sun to stand still to finish the battle

The sun stood still by Joshua asking of the Lord never again has this happened that a man so boldly asked of the Lord and he stop the sun in the sky for a day

13 Judges of Israel

Joshua died, and God anointed Judges to lead Israel

Othniel was the first of the judges to lead Israel

Othniel Caleb's younger brother was first to save them from hands of King of Aram

Ehud was next lead Israel against King of Moab

Ehud went to visit the King of Moab Eglon who was a fat man

Ehud had a double edge sword he made and strapped to his right thigh

After he presented tribute to Eglon he told him he had a secrete message for him

Ehud then went back to see the king in his chambers

Ehud then plunged the sword into his belly as he was whispering in his ear

The fat closed around the sword and it disappeared, and his bowels discharged

Ehud ran away, and it took his servants time to discover him because they thought he was going to the bathroom

Ehud escaped, and the Israelites then defeated the Moab

Shamgar son of Anath lead Israel and struck down 600 Philistines

Deborah a mother in Israel led them next

Now Deborah was a profit and defeated
Jabin King of Canaan army

Sisera lead Jabin army, Deborah had
Barack lead Israel's army and the routed
Sisera army

Sisera went to hide in a women's tent
when he fell asleep, she nailed a tent
stake through his temple then called for
Barak to come into her tent to show him
where he was hiding, and Canaan was
defeated

14 Gideon accomplished much with the few that God provided

Midian was so oppressive to Israel that
God sent them another Judge to lead

Gideon was visited by an Angel of the Lord

The Angel of the said the Lord is with you mighty warrior

Though Gideon was not there yet the Angel called it by Faith

Gideon sought proof from God and put a Fleece on the threshing floor and asked God for there to be dew not on it in the morning and only on the ground around it and it was

Then Gideon ask the opposite for the next morning and the sign was there dew only on the Fleece and it was, so he rung out the fleece and got a bowl full but none on the ground

Gideon then sent out with all his army to defeat Median

But the Lord said you have too many men and Israel will think they did this on their own

So, the Lord had him send 22000 men home

Bu that still was not enough for the Lord

So, the Lord told Gideon take the men to the water

The men who lapped like dogs were to go home and the men who drank with cupped hands were to go on

Only 300 men were left to glorify God through Gideon's army

The Lord told Gideon go up against the Midian for I have given them into your hands

Gideon told his men to split in two and when he told them to blow their trumpets

When the 300 trumpets sounded the Lord caused the medians to turn on each other with their swords and they were routed to glorify God on that day

15 Judges Continued

Abimelech was next judge he was a son of Gideon

Tola was next to judge Israel

Jair had thirty sons, who rode thirty donkeys, and controlled 30 cities in Gilead

Jephthah judged for six years

Ibzan of Bethlehem judged Israel 7 years and he had thirty sons, and thirty daughters

Elon judged Israel 10 years

Abdon had 40 sons' and 30 grandson's and ruled Israel for 8 years.

Samson was the last to Judge Israel before a Monarchy was established by God

16 Samson's Riddle

Sampson was born; Chapter 13 of Judges tells the story of Manoah and his wife who was barren an angel of the Lord appears to Manoah's wife promising that she will bear a son.

She drank no alcohol and never cut his hair because her son will be a Nazirite dedicated to the Lord from his birth.

She also learns that her son will save the Israelites from the Philistines.

When Sampson was of age his parents wanted to get him a wife.

Sampson was in love with a philistine woman, so they arranged it even though it was against God's Law and his parent tried to discourage him

But this marriage would lead to Sampson first use of his superhero strength by killing a Lion on the way to meet the wife's family

Samson then gave a riddle to the wife's family men and wagered 30 suits of clothes "out of the eater something sweat out of the eater something to eat". For when he returned to the Lion carcass it was full of bees and honey.

The men then went to his wife and asked her to find out the meaning of the riddle, so they could win the wager

After she pestered him day and night, she said he did not love her and then he told her the riddle she then told the men of her family

Then when Samson returned, the men said to him what is stronger than a lion what is sweater than honey and then he owed them 30 suits of clothes

Samson then said if you had not plowed with my Heifer you would not know, Samson then went and killed 30 Philistines and took their clothes to pay the debt

Samson then left, and his wife was given to one of his companions instead

17 Samson takes revenge

Samson then returns looking for his wife

Her father said I thought you did not want her anymore, so I gave her to your companion

Her Father then said take her sister she is younger and good looking

Samson was mad and took revenge on the Philistines for that act

He then took 30 foxes and tied their tales and lighted them on fire to run through their farm fields

The Philistines then looked to kill Samson and he allowed himself to be caught only to break free and kill some 1000 men with a Jawbone of an ass.

18 Sampson and Delia

Samson then meet a woman called
Delila

Delila then attempted to trick Samson 3
different times to tell him the secret of
his strength by tying him up

Each time he told her a lie, and she
would say Samson the Philistines are
upon you and he would break free of
the ropes just in time to fight his way
out of it

But then he told Delila after she said he
did not love her, (he fell for that again
like his first wife showing his weakness)
that the real source of his strength is his
hair that had not been cut from birth.

She then put him to sleep in her lap and her friends cut his hair when he was asleep, and then tied him up again

When he awoke, he could not break free this time from their ropes

The Philistines then gauged out his eyes

They then tied him up in their temple

During a festival to Dagon their God they mocked him and tied him to the Columns

Samson then asked God for strength one more time he pushed on the columns he was tied to and down the columns and roof of the temple fell killing more Philistines in his death than his life.

19 Ruth & Boaz's Favor

Rehab the women who helped Joshua's spies at Jericho was a Grandmother to Boaz

Ruth was a Moabite woman who was married to an Israelite man a son of Naomi

Ruth's Mother in Law name was Naomi

Ruth and Her sister-in-law husbands Naomi's sons were killed on the same day in battle

Ruth Sister in law left Naomi and went back to her people but Ruth stayed

Ruth Loved Naomi and was very loyal to her

Ruth and Naomi went back to her people; Naomi changes her name to MARA which means sorrow

Ruth and Naomi were hungry, so Ruth went to a field to pick grain

The field was Boaz's and he took notice of Ruth and told his workers to leave her extra grain for her to find easier

Ruth told Naomi and she was happy she found favor in his eyes and she said Boaz is our Kinsman redeemer (Meaning closest relative on Naomi's side who could inherit her son's property)

Naomi Told Ruth what to do put on some nice clothes and perfume and go back to threshing floor to meet Boaz

Ruth did lay down at Boaz's feet and covered herself with his blanket while he was sleeping per Naomi's instruction

When Boaz woke, he found Ruth and she told him he was her Kinsman redeemer since she lost her husband

Boaz was honored she did not go after someone younger but said there was another Kinsman, he would have to check with first

Boaz meet with their other closest Kin and said to take Ruth's husbands land he would have to marry Ruth, but he was already married and declined to Boaz

Boaz then Married Ruth and the Lived
Happily having a son Jesse and a
Grandson David who would become
King of all Israel & Judah

20 David's Faith

David was a man after God's own heart

God instructed the Profit Samuel to pick
David over David's Father Jesse 7 other
sons

The Israelites went to war and Jesse sent
David to bring supplies to his brothers

David's older brother taunted him
saying David why are you here and with

whom have you left those few sheep, trying to belittle him but David was very strong in faith and it did not sway him

Goliath was tautening the Israelite army to fight him he was over 7 ft. tall a giant man by any times standards

Saul the King said he would give his daughter in marriage to whomever could defeat him

David knew his God was bigger than any man or army

David selected 4 smooth stones and went to battle with only his sling

David believed God would defeat the Philistine Giant by Faith

David said to Goliath today I will defeat you and feed your head to the birds of the air

David took out the stone and slinged it into Goliath's forehead

David knocked out Goliath, and pulled out the Giant's sword and cut off his head

David defeated the Giant with his own sword; God raised him up in the presence of his enemies

21 Saul the Good & then Mad King

Saul was anointed by Samuel the prophet to be Israel's first king

Israel said to Samuel and God give us a King like other nations

Saul was a head taller than everyone else and looked the part of a King

At first things were good with Saul the Kingdom was expanded and was prosperous

Then after David defeated Goliath for Saul

Then one Day Saul heard the women singing after a battle Saul has killed thousands and David has killed 10's of thousands, Saul started to go Mad with Jealousy

Then Saul started to become even more crazy and one day in the Royal hall he attempted to pin David to a wall with a spear David then had to flee the Saul on many occasions

But David would not harm the Lords anointed

Saul knew then that David was the better man and had become God's anointed

Saul has once disobeyed the Lord and taken spoils of a victory after Samuel the prophet told him not to this angered the Lord prompting Samuel to anoint the son of Jesse David

Saul knew his time was numbered and David would someday rule

But David would not harm the Lords anointed, even though on not one but to occasions Saul was delivered into his hands by chance where he could have killed him

When day before a battle Saul went to Endour to a median to call up Samuels Ghost to get advice

The Median told Saul he would not have victory, but the Mad king went into battle the next Day and He and his Sons where all killed

In the Battle Saul after seeing his sons killed, he fell on his sword, and another man then ran him through with his own sword to finish him off, then ran to tell David thinking he would be rewarded for the news.

When the news reached David, he would be king, the person that ran Saul's sword through him to finish him off told the story to David. Then David said by your own words you are guilty, and David had him killed for Killing the Lords anointed, then David became King and united Israel

22 David's was a man after God' own Heart

David was anointed by Samuel to be the next king of Israel after Saul

Saul heard the woman singing this song after a battle

Saul as killed thousands David has killed tens of thousands

After that Saul was Jealous David would take his thrown and looked for a way to kill him

Saul son Jonathan was best friends with David and tried to help David

Saul attempted to spear David one day in a fit of rage in the Palace

David escaped and ended up living on the run with a band of great fighters, he assembled David's Mighty Men

Saul pursued David into the mountains and one day the Lord delivered Saul into David hands

David would not kill Saul he sneaked up behind him cutting off a corner of his rob while Saul was relieving himself in a cave alone

David and his men were hiding in the cave and Saul did not know

David showed Saul the garment from a long way off calling from a distance and Saul knew he was unjust in his pursuit of David

Another Time Saul hunted David and again the lord delivered Saul into David's hands again

This time David sneaked into Saul's camp, took Saul's spear while he was sleeping, and again David showed it to him calling from a distance

David would not kill the Lord's anointed and Saul strayed from the Lord more and more

Saul knew at this time and said David was the better man, and David now was to one day lead Israel

Saul consulted mediums in Endor and talked to a spirit calling himself Samuel who told him he would die in battle the next day

Saul died in battle the next day and a man ran to tell David that he helped finish Saul off, and David had him killed for killing the Lords anointed.

David was man after God's own heart God blessed him and become the second King of Israel after Saul's Death.

23 City of David

David and his army led by Joab son of Zurabel took back Israel & Judah from the philistines and other tribes

David settled in Jerusalem and made it his capital, the City of David.

In the spring, a time when Kings go off to war David stayed home as Joab led his army

David saw Bathsheba on her roof taking a bath one night from his palace

David fell in love with Bathsheba, invited her to the palace, and made her with Child

Uriah the Hittite was Bathsheba's Husband, he was at war with Joab and the Israelite army

David sent word for Uriah to return home from the army

Once home Uriah was invited into David's palace and David tried to get him drunk to get him to sleep with his wife in his own home

Though intoxicated Uriah would not enter his house to sleep with his wife while his army was at war, He sleep outside on the steps of his home

David tried multiple times to get Uriah to sleep with Bathsheba to cover their sin, but he would not take pleasures while his army was in battle

David sends Uriah back to Joab with sealed instructions for Joab to put him into the most dangerous part of battle and then pull back and leave him to be killed

Uriah was killed, then Nathan confronted David about his sin, and it would be against his house

Then the child became sick and David fasted and prayed and hoped the Lord would spare Bathsheba's child

David child with Bathsheba died; David's men were afraid to tell him, but he said he cannot come to me but one day I will go to him and David stopped fasting and moved on

but David and Bathsheba will have another child their second son Solomon

David's son Amnon raped his half-sister Tamar the sin of David house was being passed down for his transgression

Amnon was infatuated with Tamar and pretended to be sick and asked for Tamar to make him her bread which was his favorite, but when she brought it to his room, he raped her against her will

Tamar pleaded with him to ask for her hand in marriage, but he would not, all he knew was his on lust

After the rape he hated her and demanded she leave his sight

Absalom seeker revenge of Amnon for the rape of his beautiful sister

Absalom assonated Amnon at a party at his house for what he did to Tamar

Half the kingdom sided with Absalom and civil war broke out in Israel

David and his men had to flee to the wilderness, but they fought this kind of war before

Absalom received poor counsel from one of David advisors and decided to follow David into the wilderness

David's army and Joab set a trap for Absalom army at a river near a forest

Absalom was killed by Joab when his hair was caught in a tree while riding his mount

David mourned Absalom but encourage by his army he returned home to rule

David ruled in Jerusalem till his old age

David had paid for his sin and though his faith was great we should all learn not to cover up our sin or face the consequence of a just God

24 Solomon's Wisdom & Favor

When David was in his old age, he promised Bathsheba her son Solomon would be heir to the thrown

Solomon was Highly favored and was not blamed for his parent's mistakes

When David was old his advisors found a young beautiful girl Abishag to be David's wife to keep him warm

David could not stay warm in his old age he did not have relations with Abishag

David son Adonijah the elder tried to take Solomon's thrown

Adonjah convinced Joab and the other advisors to crown him king of Israel

Bathsheba and Nathan moved quickly to David to secure the thrown for Solomon

Solomon is crowned King by David as he was promised

Adonijah throws himself at Solomon's mercy and Solomon lets him live but warns him if he ever tries anything again surely it will be his death

Adonjah tries to marry Abishag by tricking Bathsheba to ask Solomon for her

Solomon is furious because he knows this will give him a claim on the thrown

Solomon has him killed where he stands at the horns of the altar of the Temple

David goes to be with his fathers; Solomon becomes King of Israel by God's Favor

David told Solomon to not let Joab's Gray head go down to the grave in peace, so Solomon had him killed for his betrayals of David and murders he committed in the past

God comes to Solomon asks him in a dream what he wants, and Solomon said Wisdom

God said since you did not ask for riches or long life, but Wisdom I will grant you them all no one before or after was ever wiser than Solomon

All the People, Kings, and Queens came from all around to hear Solomon's Wisdom.

25 Solomon the builder

Solomon was the wisest man ever on earth by God's favor he asked God and he granted him such wisdom

Solomon had many wise men and women who came to see him to hear his wisdom

They would all bring gifts and he accumulated much Gold and capital items to trade

Solomon took the riches God provide and built a great temple to house the Arc of the Covenant which held the original 10 commandments

His Palace also was built and there was none as ornate and of complicated construction in the world

God showed Solomon many great and ancient wisdoms of building and he showed his builders

He made treaty with the King of Lebanon to provide great Cedars to build with, Solomon was wise in these ways

The Queen of Sheba came with great wealth and gifts for Solomon just to hear him speak of this wisdom that was from God

Solomon had many wives' some say over 700

Solomon wrote down great proverbs of his wisdom keep in the Bible to this day a Wisdom of the ages

Solomon's wives ultimately lead him astray to build idles for their gods, God was not pleased but allowed him to stay on the thrown because of his love for David

Some say Solomon would have repented of this before his death because of his great wisdom the Bible does not say

Some of Solomon wisdom is with us today in proverbs & should be studied because God likes to give his children great gifts and favor

26 Kings of Israel and Juda

Approx. Date BC	Kings of Israel-Judah	Years as king /Behavior noted in Bible
1050 - 1010	Saul	40 Good then Mad king
1010 - 970	David	40 Greatest King
970 - 930	Solomon	40 Wisest King

Date	Kings of just Israel	Years as King	Rating
930 - 909	Jeroboam I	22	Did Evil in eyes of the Lord
909 - 908	Nadab	2	Did Evil in eyes of the Lord
908 - 886	Baasha	24	Did Evil in eyes of the

			Lord
886 - 885	Elah	2	Did Evil in eyes of the Lord
885	Zimri	7 days	Did Evil in eyes of the Lord
885 - 880	Tibni *	5	ok
885 - 874	Omri *	12	Not good @ all
874 - 853	Ahab	22	Worst king
853 - 852	Ahaziah	2	Did Evil in eyes of the Lord
852 - 841	Joram	12	Did Evil mostly
841 - 814	Jehu	28	Did Evil mostly
814 - 798	Jehoahaz	17	Did Evil in eyes of the Lord

798 - 782	Jehoash	16	Did Evil in eyes of the Lord
793 - 753	Jeroboam II	41	Did Evil in eyes of the Lord
753	Zechariah	6 months	Did Evil in eyes of the Lord
752	Shallum	1 month	Did Evil in eyes of the Lord
752 - 742	Menahem**	10	Did Evil in eyes of the Lord
752 - 732	Pekah**	20	Did Evil in eyes of the Lord
742 - 740	Pekahiah**	2	Did Evil in eyes of the Lord
732 - 723	Hoshea	9	Did Evil in eyes of the Lord

Date	Kings of Judah	Years as King	Rating
930 - 913	Rehoboam	17	Did Evil mostly
913 - 910	Abijah	3	Did Evil mostly
910 - 869	Asa	41	Good
872 - 848	Jehoshaphat	25	Good
853 - 841	Jehoram	8	Did Evil in eyes of the Lord
841	Ahaziah	1	Did Evil in eyes of the Lord
841 - 835	Queen Athaliah	7	Devilish
835 - 796	Joash	40	Good mostly
796 - 767	Amaziah	29	Good mostly
792 - 740	Azariah (Uzziah)	52	Good

Date	Kings of Judah	Years as King	Rating
750 - 732	Jotham	16	Good
732 - 715	Ahaz	17	Wicked
715 - 686	Hezekiah	29	A Very Good King
696 - 642	Manasseh	55	Worst
642 - 640	Amon	2	Worst
640 - 609	Josiah	31	A Very Good King
609	Jehoahaz	3 months	Did Evil in eyes of the Lord
609 - 598	Jehoiakim	11	Wicked
598 - 597	Jehoiachin	3 months	Did Evil in eyes of the Lord
597 - 586	Zedekiah	11	Did Evil in eyes of the Lord

In 597 B.C. Jerusalem falls to Nebuchadnezzar King of Babylon. Nebuchadnezzar captures Jehoiachin takes him as prisoner to Babylon. Zedekiah is set up as a king over Judah loyal to Nebuchadnezzar, but then betrays him.

In 586 B.C. Nebuchadnezzar lays siege to Jerusalem. He destroys the city and burns down the temple Solomon built for the Lord. Nebuchadnezzar Kills Zedekiah 2 sons before him and then puts out his eyes so it will be the last thing he ever sees. The then what is left of the Jews and Zedekiah are carried off to Babylon.

27 Daniel Favor and Great health

Israel was carried into captivity

Daniel and his friends were taken to Babylon

King Nebuchadnezzar renamed Daniel and his friends; Nebuchadnezzar was king of Babylonia from 605 BC to around 563 BC

The chief official gave them other names: he gave the name Belteshazzar to Daniel, Shadrach to Hananiah, Meshach to Mishael, and Abednego to Azariah.

The purpose of changing names was to help erase their attachment to their own nation

But Daniel and his friends would not change their belief

Daniel and his friends insisted on only eating Kosher vegetarian foods

They would not bend to the king officials who tried to get them to eat their unclean food

But then in turn, Daniel and his friends were healthier than all others in the Kings service

And were placed with the wise men of Babylon

They would serve the King faithfully while serving their God

They had not given up their faith, and would not bend to the king's officials who tried to get them to eat their food

They had not given up their faith and God would Bless them with his Great Favor in deeds to come in the service of the King

28 Daniel and the interpretation

King Nebuchadnezzar had a dream and asked the wise men of his court to interpret it

But first they must tell him what the dream was

the wise men had said this had never been done before or asked by any king when they would not answer the King ordered them all put to death

Daniel was told of the decree he then asked why the king would put such a harsh decree into effect

Daniel then asked the King for time to pray to God for the meaning of the dream.

God then gave Daniel the meaning of the dream while he and his friends fasted and prayed

the king saw statue made of four different metals; Nebuchadnezzar's was the head of gold, implying it was a golden age, or time of prosperity

The head was made of gold, the torso of silver, the stomach and upper legs of bronze, and the legs of iron, with some clay mixed in for the feet.

a stone was bashed into the feet of it, causing the clay to break and the statue to collapse, leaving just the stone in its place.

The bronze layer was the Median-Persian Empire, during which the Judeans returned from exile. The, the stomach and upper legs of bronze is Greece, or the Hellenistic Empire of Alexander the Great, as it begins strong, then becomes mixed with clay, representative of the kingdom being split after Alexander the Great's death.

the legs of iron, with some clay mixed in for the feet; is the Roman empire of old antiquity, and the new one that is yet to come.

The stone that breaks the statue "not by human hands" and becomes a mountain that overtakes the earth is Israel reunited and placed in power by God, possible interpretation is the second coming of Jesus Christ

29 Daniel and the Lion's den

After Daniel had gained such Favor for interpreting the King's dream, Nebuchadnezzar's made him Chief wise man

The wise men were jealous, so they looked for ways to trip up Daniel

They made a rule no one could pray to their God; only worship the King and they made a royal decree that could not be broken

When Daniel was caught praying to his God he was brought before the king

Remember in ancient times the Kings Law could not be changed

So, the king sentenced Daniel to the Lion's Den, if innocent he would be delivered from it unharmed

Daniel prayed his God would deliver him

He was thrown into to the Lion's den for a night

The next morning the king ran to the lion's den

The King called Daniel my friend is you ok

Daniel said yes, the God of my Fathers has delivered me

No matter how great the tragedy

The king then ordered the wise men wo accused Daniel to be thrown into the lions

They were torn from limb to limb immediately

This shows that through great faith we all can be delivered, anything is possible

30 Nebuchadnezzar's makes a statue

Nebuchadnezzar's makes a statue of himself and commands everyone to bow down to it

But Shadrach, Meshach, and Abednego the 3 Hebrew young wise men Daniel's Friends would not

This makes the King angry and he orders them thrown into the furnace

He orders the furnace be made 7 times hotter than normal

When the soldiers throw the young men into the furnace, they catch on fire it is so hot

But the 3 young Jews are not burnt

Then the king looks in and said we threw in 3 men into the furnace but there are now 4 and one looks like the son of God walking around

The 3 young men walk out unharmed

Even their clothes did not smell of smoke God had protected them so

the King then ordered all his empire going forward to worship the God of Shadrach, Meshach, and Abednego

31 Queen Esther Highly Favored

King Xerxes was in his Court and called Queen Vashti in

She refused to be summoned

His wise men then advised him to do something or all the men would suffer the same disrespect from their wives

So, the King then ordered Queen Vashti to never come in his site again, and removed her title

A search was then set out for a new queen, the most beautiful women were gathered to undergo beauty treatments

Mortdecai the Jew and guardian of Esther encourage her to try for Queen

After she had beauty treatments she then was brought before the King

He could not take his eyes off her and with God's favor she was picked to be Queen

Mortdecai one day overheard a plot to kill the King

Mortdecai then told Esther who told the King and he was saved from the plot against his life

Haman was second to the King in power

Mortdecai was a Jew and there for would not bow to Haman when he came through the city gate

Haman then tricked the King to make a Law that the Jews would be killed on the 15th day of the 12 months

Mortdecai found out and said to Esther she must tell the king

She did not want to tell the King, but Mortdecai said that it was for a time just like this that she was given this Favor of being a Queen and if she did not do something God would raise someone else for it

32 Esther Time had come for her purpose to be revealed

Mortdecai insisted Esther help the Jews and speak to the King

Esther then approached the King and he extended out his scepter for it was Death to approach the king without being summoned

Esther then approaching the King asked for him to come to Dinner with her, and invited Haman

The King agreed and said to ask for up to half of his Kingdom and he would grant it, but she just had a dinner planned at first.

At the Dinner the King told her to ask for whatever she wanted again she said for the King and Haman to come to dinner again tomorrow.

The King could not sleep and asked for the books from his court to be read.

He read about the good deed Mordecai did to save him.

He then asks Haman what to do to honor a man who the King wanted to honor, and Haman being Vain thought it was him; so, he suggested to put a royal robe on him and go up and down the streets proclaiming this is what the king does to those he wants to honor.

The King said good to Haman now go and honor Mordecai.

Mordecai did as tell, but when he was done, he made a Gallows to impale Mordecai on when it was time to kill the Jews.

The time of Esther's dinner came, and the King asked again what she wanted.

This time she said her life and revealed she was a Jew and Haman had a plan to kill all the Jews approved by the King.

The King then left in anger from the room.

Haman knowing the king had already made up his mind through himself at Esther feet to plead for his life

At that time the king came back in and found Haman touching Esther

The King said to his men to Have Haman killed on the very Gallows he built for Mordecai

Then Mordecai was made 2nd to King as an adviser; for he and Esther were loyal and highly favored by God and then His King.

33 Job a tale for all to remember in a time of trial

Job was one of the wealthiest men in all Israel and the world.

Job was righteous before God and Humble.

one day Satan went to God to discuss the Earth and God asked him to consider his servant Job.

Satan said let me take away His wealth and family and he will surely curse God.

God agreed but added he was not to hurt job.

Satan then took away Job's thousands of Camels, Sheep, Cows, and animals.

He also had his Sons and Daughters killed while they were having a party by a great wind that came and collapsed the house.

Only Job and his wife remind alive but were destitute.

Job has 3 friends come to visit and the wonder what he did wrong to deserve this fate.

But Job had done nothing to deserve it and he would not curse God he just was living in a fallen world manipulated by evil.

After many months of suffering and Job getting boils and skin diseases, he still will not curve God and his 3 friends blame him for his troubles.

But when God reveals himself to Job, he said his friends were wrong to accuse him of being responsible for his poverty and poor health and said if Job would make an offering for friends, he would forgive them.

So, Job then made a suitable offering and his friends, and they were forgiven.

Afterwards Job asked God for forgiveness of questioning him for his situation.

God then restores double back to Job for all his troubles and brings him out of poverty into great wealth & riches and flocks and herds and restores his health to normal

Job lives to be 140 years old and see to the 4 generation of grand children

Job had 7 more sons and 3 of the most beautiful daughters the earth had ever seen, there is no limit to God's favor when we believe that our due season will come

We live in a fallen world and bad things happen to good people, but it is all part of God's greater plan for Good, and our development into the person he can use to better his Kingdom.

34 Job's Wisdom

The words of Job are true through the wisdom of the ages; Mortals born of woman, are of few days and full of trouble.

Men & Women They spring up like flowers and wither away; like fleeting shadows, they do not endure.

Do you (The Lord) fix your eye on them?
Will you bring them before you for
judgment?

Who can bring what is pure from the
impure? No one; Meaning who can
make man pure only God

A person's days are determined; you
have decreed the number of his months
and have set limits he cannot exceed.
(this is something Solomon refers to in
ECCl. That are days are numbered and
we need to enjoy our lot of days', our
work under the sun).

So, look away from him and let him alone, till he has put in his time like a hired laborer. We are all here to labor on and enjoy that labor each man & woman is given is his lot in life make the most of it, and enjoy your work, your lot in your life, your family, your job, your free time, and being blessed by God and being a blessing to others.

35 Elijah and Elisha

Elijah was a profit in Israel

Elijah did many miracles and God showed him incredible Favor maybe more than anyone in the Bible

Elijah could call fire down from Heaven

Elijah could call Legion of the Lords Host to Fight for him and Kill Israel's enemies

Elijah could end droughts with his Faith and Favor

Elijah was a servant of God but always believed that God gave him the power to do miracles

Elijah had a servant Elisha

Elisha was a faithful servant to his master and would not leave his side

When Elijah knew his time was short and all the profits were saying he would leave this world today

Elisha asked for a double portion of Elijah spirit

Elijah said what you ask is a hard thing, but if you see me taken up to heaven today you will receive it

Elisha saw his master taken up to heave in a fiery chariot and he did receive a double portion of his spirit doing twice as many miracles in his lifetime.

36 <u>Elijah's 8 miracles he did;</u> some of the miracles are interpreted differently by other scholars but this will give the basic stories of them.

1. Shut up the heavens causing a drought 1 Kings 17:1

2. Multiplied flour and oil for a starving widow and her son 1 Kings 17:14-16

3. Raised the widow's son from the dead 1 Kings 17:22-23

4. Defeated the prophets of Baal with fire he called sown from heaven 1 Kings 18:25-38

5. Brought rain to end the drought in Israel 1 Kings 18:41-45

6. Destroyed 50 Soldiers and Commander with fire and lightening 2 Kings 1:9-10

7. Destroyed another 50 Soldiers and Commander soldiers with fire and lightening 2 Kings 1:11-12

8. Parted the waters of the Jordan River 2 Kings 2:8

37 Elisha's 16 miracles

1. Parted the waters of the Jordan River with Elijah's cloak 2 Kings 2:14

2. Purified water to drink 2 Kings 2:19-22

3. Called in bears to ravage young men who harassed him 2 Kings 2:23-24

4. Caused a flood to save Israel from the Moabites 2 Kings 3:14-25

5. Made a miraculous flow of oil for a poor starving widow 2 Kings 4:2-7

6. Gave fertility to the woman of Shunem whom he stayed with

sometimes in her spare room2 Kings 4:8-17

7. Raised a child from the dead he loved "the all is well story" 2 Kings 4:32-37

8. Purified poisoned soup to save people 2 Kings 4:38-41

9. Multiplied loaves to feed a large crowd of people 2 Kings 4:42-44

10. Healed Naaman of leprosy by dunking in the Jordon River 7 times 2 Kings 5:1-19

11. Gehazi he cursed with leprosy for disobeying him and taking payment for the miracle of Naaman 2 Kings 5:20-27

12. Made an iron axe head float for those who lost it but could not afford another 2 Kings 6:1-7

13. Struck the Aramaeans blind so they could not see him 2 Kings 6:18

14. Predicted the end of the Aramaean siege 2 Kings 7:1-20

15. Predicted the death of Ben-Hadad and the rise of Hazael 2 Kings 8:7-15

16. Raised a man from the dead after his death when he was thrown into Elisha's grave and touched his bones, then the fallen soldier came back to life

Each one of these miracles are a story in themselves but that is was the Bible chapter is listed if you wish to learn more.

38 70 years of Captivity

587 BCE. Nebuchadnezzar destroyed the Jerusalem city wall and the Temple, Zedekiah and his sons

After the sack of Jerusalem Zedekiah was looking on, his 2 sons were put to death; Then Nebuchadnezzar had Zedekiah's eyes put out, placed him in chains, and took him to Babylon

Then began 70 years of captivity in Babylon empire

During this time, we had the stories of Daniel and Nebuchadnezzar, and Queen Esther and Xerxes

According to the book of Ezra, the Persian King Cyrus ended the exile in 538 BCE,

Ezra was given the money from the royal treasury to go back and rebuild the city.

There were many in opposition like Sanballat and Tobiah and the Arabs and the Ammonites and the Ashdodites heard that the repairing of the walls of Jerusalem were beginning to be closed, they were very angry; and they all plotted together to come and fight against Jerusalem

These are hard times to understand in the bible and take many readings spread across many books

But the stories, of Daniel, Queen Esther, Nebuchadnezzar, Xerxes, Cyrus, Ezra, and Nehemiah all books ty together

As well as the book of Kings ty in and tell these stories of God allowing this to happen because Israel stopped following him

But when they returned to his following God, they once again regained his favor and returned to the promised land

But under Nehemiah the Israel families return to Jerusalem to re-settle

According to the book of Ezra, the Persian King Cyrus ended the exile in 538 BCE,

These are hard times to understand in the bible and take many readings spread across many books

39 Remember Israel's Captivity

All these stories of captivity are meant to be a learning tool. An ancient wisdom

Remember the past and how we failed and did not accept God's Favor

Favor is a gift like eternal life in the New Testament.

Favor is ours if we accept it God wants us to have his Favor

 I do not presume what happens after death just that we all will face it

God wants us to have a good life and be blessed

It is when we reject his ways and wisdom and try to do it on our own that we lose it

If you try to do things as much as you can his way; he understands we will fail but then he will bless us with a just life and the ability to pursue our happiness and receive his blessings both spiritual and financial on Earth and spiritual after death.

I prefer to face life with the thought of eternal life as a gift

And I enjoy his gift of favor on Earth each day while we have it

Remember just accepting it and attempting to believe in his teachings will bring favor to you & generations of your family by your faith, I have seen it and it is buried in these stories from the Bible and in God's words. But you must study it and accept it, and try and fail, but then you can and will receive.

40 Ecclesiastes

Christmas day reading Ecclesiastes written by the wisest men who ever lived.

I realized that each man lot in life is his or her own pleasures of Work, Family, Life, and their time on the earth.

There is an ancient wisdom in these words that I wanted to share a History of mankind that ties us all together with past present and future to show us how to live our lives and to get the most enjoyment and fulfillment from it.

 I write this brief history of the Bible for my purposes and hope you find some use of it. Our creator gave us this book of wisdom to help us understand the mysteries of our lives and others. To everything there is a time and a season, this is our season for Wisdom, Health and favor you need only to understand what power you have through belief and it will be all tied together

Ecclesiastes everything is meaningless

What do we gain from our time under the sun?

Generation come and go like family members at Christmas past in our mind

We never have enough or can get enough

What has been will be again and there is
nothing new

I have wanted things and built them for
my self

Houses, Homes, Gold, Vineyards and
land I have

It is all meaningless but our work our lot
in life our work under the sun

I denied myself no pleasure

I will work my whole life just to leave it
to someone

My heir may be good or bad it is
meaningless

The fate of a fool will overtake him

The wise and the fool the same
overtakes them both so what is real

A person can do nothing better to eat and drink and find satisfaction in their own work

To the person who pleases him God gives wisdom, knowledge and happiness

To the sinner or fool he gives a task of gathering up wealth and storing it

Then he gives that wealth to those who please him

This is God's Favor for those who believe

So, believe and take pleasure in your work and your lot in life your family and time

To the person who pleases him God gives wisdom, knowledge and happiness, and sometimes we have peace in this world for a little while this

is a gift from God and every day is Grace
enjoy it.

Final Word

These Bible stories are not all listed in
their entirety but are just a Bible History
101 version of what I felt the top 40
stories everyone should know. I
encourage you to read the Bible I have
been reading it for 20 years I try to read
it in its entirety once per year, it is how I

learned this Old Testament History so well and found wisdom and knowledge in its teaching. I encourage you to find a Bible based church to study with if you are able, but if you cannot study on the internet or listen to shows like Joel Osteen's weekly programing, I found it encouraging. There is no wrong way to learn these stories it is like reading about anything you may have a passion for just start reading & learning and it will come to you eventually and start to make more sense about the world around you and your role in it.

<u>**References:**</u>

King James Bible Old Testament

New King James Bible Old Testament

NIV Bible Old Testament

Biblestudy.org for Key dates on kings of Judah and Israel

BibleGateway.com for different versions of Bible Interpretations.